the little book of
LOVE

the little book of
LOVE

Glenda Timms

ARCTURUS

PICTURE CREDITS

Corbis: 10 (Ariel Skelley), 16 (Horst Ossinger/dpa), 20 (Templer/Corbis), 24 (Fabio Cardoso), 25 (Rainer Jensen/dpa), 26 (Tim Davis), 27 (Jenny E. Ross), 28 (Klick/Radius Images), 30 (Frans Lanting), 31 (Karen Huntt), 34 (A. Inden), 36 (China Daily/Reuters), 38 (Ronnie Kaufman), 39 (Paul Souders), 41 (Daniel J. Cox), 54 (Renee Lynn), 57 (Ariel Skelley), 59 (Daniel J. Cox), 61 (Roy Morsch), 62 (Ariel Skelley), 66 (Hill Street Studios/Blend Images LLC), 70 (Ron Watts), 77 (John Henley), 80 (Paul Barton), 85 (Roy McMahon), 87 (Keren Su), 89 (ZUMA Press), 93 (Don Johnston/All Canada Photos) **Shutterstock:** cover, 6, 7, 8, 9, 11, 13, 14, 15, 17, 18, 19, 21, 22, 23, 29, 32, 33, 35, 37, 40, 42, 44, 45, 46, 47, 48, 49, 50, 51, 52, 53, 55, 56, 58, 60, 63, 64, 65, 67, 68, 69, 71, 72, 73, 74, 75, 76, 78, 79, 81, 83, 84, 86, 88, 90, 91, 92, 94, 95, 96 **Press Association:** 12 (Demotix/Press Association Images), 43 (AP/Press Association Images), 82 (APA/Roland Schlager)

ARCTURUS

This edition published in 2012 by Arcturus Publishing Limited
26/27 Bickels Yard, 151–153 Bermondsey Street,
London SE1 3HA

Copyright © 2012 Arcturus Publishing Limited

ISBN: 978-1-84858-371-9
AD002058EN

Printed in China

What is love? We all know it when we feel it, but who can truly define it? Love comes in so many forms and affects us in a multitude of ways, some blissful, some agonizing.

Sometimes it burns and smoulders like a volcano, a passionate rush of raw emotion; but the love that warms us gently, almost without our knowing it's there, is every bit as powerful – and we miss it just as much when it is gone.

Love is a flame that likes to be fanned. If you love somebody, let them know.

Love makes us feel warm and full of joy.

Sometimes just being together is enough.

It makes us revel in our surroundings.

And throw ourselves into the river of life.

Love encourages us to make the most of the good times.

True love makes relaxing with each other extra-special.

Love turns our strength into gentleness.

Love is not hurried, but patient and committed.

It makes us tolerant and forgiving.

It's amazing what we'll put up with for love.

Love makes us happy to share our pleasures.

As well as life's ups and downs.

There's twice the joy in doing things with your other half.

Life's a stroll with the one you adore.

And nights out together are special.

True love lasts through the autumn of our years.

It all begins when you meet a soul mate

Some like to make the partnership official.

But true love stands the test of time.

And while the spirit's willing, anything is possible!

A parent's love wraps us up like a protective blanket.

We can feel love's warmth even in the harshest conditions.

And as we receive love, so we learn to pass it on.

We know who we can lean on when times are hard.

And who to go to for a reassuring hug.

We go to great lengths to make ourselves look lovable.

Never forget the gifts nature gave you.

Certain gestures can leave us helpless.

We try to make ourselves irresistible in many ways.

Sometimes we don't even have to try that hard.

The urge for physical contact can be so powerful.

True strength comes from holding the one we love.

The warm embrace that tells us we can conquer the world.

The soft luxury of clutching them to our heart.

The heavenly tenderness of skin on loving skin.

Sometimes we like a bit of rough and tumble.

The urge to show affection can come quite out of the blue.

Even when we're on our own!

We abandon all common sense and let passion run wild.

And the results are there for all to see!

When love gets physical, anything goes.

We claim one another, and love to be claimed.

It may not be the subtlest display of affection.

We can get into all sorts of contortions.

So be careful not to overdo it.

Love does not need to be delivered with great force.

Love's light touch can feel just as strong.

And give us strength.

Delicacy is part of its power.

That easy confidence that comes with tenderness.

Love does not need to be proclaimed from the rooftops.

Just being together is enough.

Nothing's more relaxing than that comfortable silence.

When your mind's at rest and your hearts beat together.

Just close your eyes and feel the love.

Ah, romance! The spontaneous expression of true love.

The gestures that never grow stale.

Romance is the seizing of a moment.

And showing your fancy moves.

Always put your best foot forward.

Is it love that elevates mortals to the status of gods?

That makes us sacrifice all for our country… even our dignity?

That places untold meaning in inanimate objects?

That puts another higher than ourselves?

Or puts ourselves higher than all others!

Love is out there for everyone, in some shape or form.

Keep looking and you'll find your perfect match.

Body language is a clue.

And a shared sense of style.

But it's the differences that really draw us together.

Love gives us the patience to wait for another's signal.

The selflessness to do the undesirable.

The diligence to seek out the undetectable.

The confidence that no one will come between you.

And the loyalty to support the unsupportable.

Love isn't always a two-way thing.

Sometimes you have to accept it's time to give up.

We all have times when we'd rather be left alone.

And short distances begin to seem like miles.

The more desperate we get for love,
the more it seems to shun us.

We all know that look of lost love.

The utter despondency of finding ourselves alone.

Parting is such sweet sorrow.

home is where
the heart is...

The longing can drive us mad.

**Though sometimes we pretend to be sad,
just to bring them crawling back.**

The pursuit of love makes optimists of us all.

Even if that hope may look a little forlorn to others.

And may even seem a bit desperate at times.

The thought of romance brings out the best in all of us.

And keeps the flame of love alight.